Been & Seen
Renfrewshire

Published in Scotland by: Been & Seen Publishing

Postal address: P.O. Box 821
Gourock
Renfrewshire
PA19 1LP
Scotland

ISBN 1 899351 00 0

A CIP catalogue record for this book is available
from the British Library

Been & Seen Concept and Design Copyright © 1994 by Tony Stewart
Printed in Scotland by Cambus Litho Ltd
Typeset by Whitelaw & Palmer

Acknowledgments

Chris Adams
for research and compilation
Jennifer Clark
for compilation
Saskia Maus
for inspiration
Peter Alexander Michael
for building illustrations
Craig Peacock
for cover, route overviews and
other illustrations
Archie Birt
for grammar
The District Councils of:
Eastwood
Inverclyde
Renfrew
Members of the Renfrewshire
Tourism Management Group
and
Renfrewshire Enterprise
without whose financial backing and
support this project would not
have been possible.

Welcome to Renfrewshire!

If you'd like to learn something new about our thriving county, then this is the place to start. In this guide book you will find 35 places of interest, ranging across the three districts of Eastwood, Inverclyde and Renfrew, and in the course of visiting them, you will soon become aware of the diversity which makes Renfrewshire unique.

Whether it be the shipbuilding and maritime traditions of Greenock and Port Glasgow, the ancient shires of Eaglesham and Newton Mearns, the majesty of Paisley Abbey, or the humble weaver's cottage in Kilbarchan, Renfrewshire represents 226 square miles of ever changing contrast. Its local heroes range from William Wallace to James Watt, its graveyards contain memorials to both Covenanter and Crusader, its recorded heritage reaches back to the 8th Century Kingdom of Dalriada and on through the Norman Noblemen to become the cradle of the great Stewart Dynasty. Its religious history predates Christendom, as the folk tales and songs of the little Renfrewshire villages show, and centuries later, it was the ordinary villagers themselves who became the heroes in the verse of Robert Pollock, one of the county's best loved poets.

But Renfrewshire offers much more than the past. With its lush rolling farmland, bordered by wild moor and intertwined by fine river and loch, the county is a haven for a panoply of wildlife. With its wonderful panoramic views over the Clyde Estuary to the purple hills of Cowal and the high peaks to the North, it boasts some of the finest scenery in Scotland. But most remarkably, it manages to combine these wonderful natural resources with an economic base that is the envy of the rest of the country. With only 7% of Scotland's population it provides a remarkable one third of the country's manufactured exports, the bulk of this being in the electronics sector. With its major road and rail networks and the burgeoning Glasgow International Airport, Renfrewshire is uniquely placed to answer the challenges which the 21st Century will soon pose.

This book, then, will take you from the vibrant arts centre at the heart of a town to the serenity of a picturesque conservation village, from the leafy shade of an old kirk cemetery to the thrills of an adventure playground in a magical country park, each step of the way laid out simply for you to follow, with each of the three routes chosen to show as much of Renfrewshire's countryside as possible. So whether your interests are historical or archeological, ornithological or hopelessly illogical, you'll be all the richer for having Been and Seen Renfrewshire.

Tony Cassidy
Chief Executive
Renfrewshire Enterprise

Contents

On behalf of the District Council I have pleasure in commending to you the various locations which feature in Been & Seen Renfrewshire. Eastwood's green and pleasant environment has long been recognised as a popular venue for day trippers. For decades Rouken Glen Park has attracted visitors from all over West Central Scotland and continues today to provide an array of excellent features and facilities including the renowned Butterfly Kingdom. Rouken Glen is also home to the biennial Artsfeast.

No trip to Eastwood would be complete without a visit to the historic village of Eaglesham which exemplifies the benefits to be derived from well thought out conservation policies.

Indeed Eastwood has a rich local history as will be seen from the venues such as Mearns Kirk, Mearns Castle and Eastwood House. The District is fortunate, too, in that it has the National Trust's impressive Greenbank House with its splendid gardens.

I do hope that you enjoy our compact and interesting circuit of venues.

Provost Leslie M. Rosin
Eastwood District Council

EASTWOOD HOUSE*

Not many District Council Offices can boast such pleasant surroundings as the leafy splendour of Eastwood Park. Such is the charm of this particular spot, in fact, that the estate was once a favourite destination of Royalty.

We know that the Kirkstyle of Eastwood was providing revenue for the choristers of Paisley Abbey as far back as the 13th Century, but from then until the late 1400s, when it came into the possession of the Montgomery family, the Barony remains shrouded in mystery. It appears from names like Brocklees, Birkenshaw and Orchard Park that a large area of the estate was woodland, probably for hunting, and there are references to charters in the succeeding centuries requiring this to be safeguarded. During this time the family seat was Corslie Castle, which reputedly stood near the present site of Woodfarm Sports Hall, but by the end of the 17th century it too had slipped into the past.

A century later much of the woodland had been uprooted and put to the

plough, and that process continued apace after 1812 when the Earl of Eglinton sold the Barony to pay for the Glasgow to Paisley Canal. The new owners split the estate up and what is now Eastwood Park was bought by the Glasgow merchant Thomas Smith in 1845. It was he who built the present house, described as 'a solid Victorian mansion, not over large, opulent without ostentation', but it was to change hands regularly over the next sixty years before its most famous occupant arrived to change its fortunes.

The future Viscount Weir purchased Eastwood Park just before the Great War which did much to make his name, and saw him promoted in 1915 to the office of Secretary of State for Air. But it was during the inter war years that Eastwood House scaled the social heights, with its owner welcoming a constant stream of the great and good of the British Establishment. So as Stanley Baldwin rubbed shoulders with General Smuts and the Duke of Windsor chatted with the Aga Khan, one might have regularly noticed the Royal Train parked just down the road at Whitecraigs Station, as Weir played host to King George V and Queen Mary.

When Weir died in 1959 the estate passed to his son, but since 1967 it has been in the hands of the local authority. In 1980 Eastwood District Council headquarters were established here. Also in the grounds you will find a theatre, swimming baths, a secondary school, and of course Eastwood House itself, now used for public and private functions.

Q. Which animals head adorns the shield above the main entrance?

Route:
Exiting Eastwood House turn right onto Rouken Glen Road. Turn right (3rd exit) at roundabout into Spiersbridge Road. Half a mile down this road on the right hand side you will find the next venue on the Eastwood District Route, Thornliebank Library.

Thornliebank Library

Having a reputation as a philanthropist and his child employees working an eighty hour week, might appear to make a man something of a moral contortionist, but such was the hard reality of Victorian values. Thornliebank owes its existence to the Crum family, for it was they who began the first successful calico printing works near what had previously been no more than a small row of cottages. This was at the beginning of the 19th century, and by 1845 the Crums were employing over 800 workers on wages of around seven shillings per week in a process which involved bleaching, finishing and power loom weaving, as well as calico printing. Business boomed under Walter Crum and when he died in 1867 he left close on £80,000, plus property worth over £120,000, and had entertained the future King Edward VII as his house guest.

It is his son Alexander, however, who gained the reputation for philanthropy, and it is he who is commemorated in the stone wall of Thornliebank's wonderfully quaint little library. Certainly some of his deeds were good... a new sewerage system for the village, rows of red brick houses noted for their surprisingly high quality and a village doctor, all reflected in the fact that Thornliebank's workforce was healthier than most. However, it is also true that the paradigm of New Lanark had demonstrated how improvements in workers' living conditions went hand in hand with higher productivity, so whether Crum Jr's motivation for being an 'enlightened employer' was driven by more than self interest is a moot point.

The library itself was built with subscriptions raised by the people of Thornliebank to commemorate their late employer, who had died one morning in 1893 on the platform of the local railway station while waiting for the 10.09 to Glasgow. Designed by Sir Roland Anderson of Edinburgh in what was described as Scottish Renaissance style, the Crum Memorial Library (to give it its full title) stood opposite the gate of the old printworks. Opened in 1896, with a stock of 2000 books, the words 'Free Library' are engraved above the door. Nowadays the printworks are long gone, as is the Crum empire, but the citizens of Thornliebank still have their library.

Open Mon, Wed, Fri, 2-5 pm and 6-8 pm. Thurs & Sat, 10 am-12.30 pm and 2-5 pm.

Q. What is the inscription above the left hand window?

Route:
Exiting Thornliebank Library turn right down Thornliebank Main Street. Turn right at first full set of traffic lights into Orchard Park Avenue. At traffic lights at T junction turn left into Fenwick Road. Take right hand lane, pass Safeway, & turn right at traffic lights into Braidholm Road, which veers hard left after 100 metres. Turn right (2nd exit) at 1st roundabout into Muirend Road. At traffic lights at T- junction turn right into Clarkston Road. Fifth left, just before tenement block is Linn Park Avenue, 100 metres down this road you will find the signpost for the next venue on the Eastwood District Route, the White Cart Walkway.

WHITE CART WALKWAY

Some of the most delightfully secluded spots in all of Eastwood can be found just a stone's throw from the bustling activity of Clarkston Road as the White Cart meanders its way down through the suburbs of Netherlee and Stamperland. Now with the advent of a new river walkway those delights have suddenly become accessible to all.

It takes only a few brief minutes for the sound of traffic to be drowned by the gurgling of water as the river makes its presence felt, and suddenly you're in a world of abundant nature, where bird, fish and insect thrive in an unbroken food chain. Dippers submerge, dislodging Mayfly nymphs from beneath the stones. Brown Trout and Salmon swim in clear fresh water. American Wild Mink and Otter have returned, and both thrive in this habitat, while along the wooded banks grow a profusion of Butterbur, Giant Bellflowers and Hart's Tongue Fern.

But it was not always thus, for the Industrial Revolution claimed this part of the river as early as the late 18th Century, with a paper mill at Netherlee using the water power to drive hammers and to pulp rags. By the 1830s the mill had become a printfield employing upwards of 250 people, with industrial property occupying more than 300 metres of the river bank. Production continued till the 1880s, with all the pollution that implies, and when the complex finally closed, it lay derelict for another eighty years before the bulldozers finally moved in.

Now nature has again reclaimed its rightful place swallowing all but the barest traces of the industrial past. So as you sit in the open picnic area drinking in the scent of wild rose and honeysuckle with your iced lemonade and cucumber sandwiches, let the sense of peace flow through you; and if you cross your fingers you may just be lucky enough to glimpse the flight of the heron as it sweeps down through the dark green canopy towards the softly gurgling waters of the Cart.

Q. What bird is the symbol of the Cart River Valley Project?

Route:
Exiting Linn Park Avenue turn left into Clarkston Road. Follow main road till you reach a roundabout. Take first exit, move into the right hand lane and turn right just before pedestrian crossing into Mearns Road. Proceed 1 mile then turn left into Flenders Road following sign for Greenbank Garden which is the next venue on the Eastwood District Route.

GREENBANK HOUSE and GARDEN*

Set in a quiet neuk of countryside behind the suburban estates of Newton Mearns, Greenbank Garden demonstrates aspects of layout and planning which should interest anyone aspiring to join the green-fingered brigade.

Greenbank House dates from 1763 and was originally built as the home of Glasgow merchant Robert Allason. A fine example of Georgian architecture, it was in the hands of one family for over 160 years and, with the exception of a Victorian porch on its south side, has remained relatively unchanged. It was gifted with its land to the National Trust for Scotland in 1961 by the then owner Mr. WP Blyth.

The property, which extends to 16 acres, contains over 2400 species of plants, (most of which would be readily available in commercial garden centres), and includes two paddocks and over 2 acres of walled garden. This garden is as old as the house itself and originally would have been used almost entirely to produce fruit and vegetables. Its layout is traditional, broad grass paths forming a cross with an old sundial at the centre of the axis. Known as the 'Scottish Lectern' sundial, this predates the house, the best estimate of its construction being circa 1620. Standing here you can see the woodland which shelters the house on three sides and to the North, a fine American Redwood peeping out.

The walled garden is itself divided into smaller plots separated by tall hedges, so that each has its own quiet space. In one you will find a pond, with a central sculpture titled 'Foam', which once graced the Empire Exhibition of 1938 at Bellahouston Park. Different aspects of this surreal female figure emerge as you circle it, always kept at bay by the water, and the thought occurs that this distance somehow symbolises the sculpture's subject... intangibility. On a less ethereal water level is the old yard pump gushing away on the opposite side of the Garden, the work of some long forgotten Busby plumber. Greenbank also has some Highland cattle on show and a woodland walk.

Q. The 100 foot high beech tree felled in 1991 was shown on a map of which year?

Open all year 9.30 am till sunset. Adults £2.00, Concessions £1.00, National Trust members free.

Route:
Exiting Greenbank, return down Flenders Road to T-junction. Turn left into Mearns Road. Take third left into Broom Road East. Immediately after Mearns Castle High School turn right into small lane signposted Maxwell Mearns Castle Parish Church. The next venue on the Eastwood District Route, Mearns Castle, is at the bottom of the lane.

MEARNS CASTLE

Not many medieval fortresses finish up as the bell tower for the local Church of Scotland, but through the centuries Mearns Castle has had a habit of swinging between the sacred and profane.

The thickly wooded knoll known as Rob's Bluff is a natural site for a fortification, defended as it is on three sides by landfall, its rocky promontory commanding a panoramic view of the surrounding country-side. The first castle here was a wooden structure built in the 1100s by Roland de Mearns, one of the Normans who had come North with Walter Fitzalan, and in those dangerous times, both William Wallace and the English King Edward I are reputed to have visited it. By the 13th century it and the surrounding buildings had become known as the 'Auld Ton' (town), and so when in due course it was replaced by the present stone structure, it was only natural that this should become the 'Newton', hence Newton Mearns.

The present castle was erected around 1450 and its builder was Sir Herbert, Lord Maxwell, a border nobleman who had gained the lands through marriage, and who was in the habit of retreating here when things got too hot in his own backyard. With its eight foot thick walls, gun slits and drawbridge over an artificial ditch, it would have made a formidable hideaway for the noble lord, but behind its grim exterior the high vaulted first floor hall contained its own minstrel's gallery, so no doubt the lute and lyre helped Sir Herbert and his minions pass many a rainy Renfrewshire winter's night.

Quite a different tune was being played by the time of the Covenanters when the castle was used by the dissenters for their religious meetings, and it was probably this which prompted the King to garrison a company of dragoons there. They not only terrorised the local population, who had moved their conventicles to the nearby moors, but before finally leaving they vandalised the castle as well. Most reports after the 18th century describe the structure as a ruin, and so it remained until the early 1970s when a little quirk of fate swung the pendulum back in favour of the powers of good.

Not far away, in the city of Glasgow, the construction of the giant Kingston Bridge had meant the demolition of the Maxwell Church, (dedicated to that same noble family). As recompense, Glasgow's Council agreed to pay for a replacement, and so the new Church was built incorporating the original tower that Sir Herbert had built more than five centuries before, and in the process guaranteeing its continued existence.

Q. A simple bench outside the castle commemorates one of the church's parishioners. What was his name?

Route:
Exiting Mearns Castle, turn left into Broom Road East, then first right into Waterfoot Road. Continue into village of Waterfoot, then turn right at cross roads into Eaglesham Road, 2 miles along this road you will find the next venue on the Eastwood District Route, the preservation village of Eaglesham.

EAGLESHAM*

Walking though the delightful village of Eaglesham, it is tempting to imagine this habitat naturally evolving over the centuries round its unique central green, a miniature wooded valley through which runs the Linn Burn. But the temptation should be resisted, for the fact is that Eaglesham is one of the first examples of the Scottish planned villages movement.

The small kirktoun of Eaglesham in the mid 18th Century held only twenty five houses, while dotted all around the surrounding countryside was a succession of fermtouns, collections of cottages that had sprung up round farms, housing mostly agricultural labourers and a few tradesmen, like blacksmiths and wheelwrights. But just around the corner was the Agricultural Revolution, and the 10th Earl of Eglinton, had recently returned from Italy where he had seen the new Planned Village in action. Needless to say, Eaglesham was next.

It took the 10th Earl three years to overcome the local hostility to the scheme, but as is the way with fait accompli, the workers finally came round to his way of thinking. 900 year leases were provided for each area of ground, and firm guidelines were laid down as to building standards, each house flush with its neighbour, the two main streets converging at the top of the Orry, as the Green was known, with a connecting path between them, so that slowly but surely the village assumed the shape of an 'A' which, coincidentally, was the Earl's first initial.

Unfortunately, the grand architect of the scheme died before completion, shot by a poacher on his Ardrossan estate, and it fell to his brother to complete the task, which he did with relish. And so we have the planned village in all its glory, probably unique in the sense that it has not been swallowed by later development. For this we have to thank a later laird of the estates, in this case the rather less grand sounding Alan Gilmour. His contribution to Eaglesham's conservation was to refuse to let the railway in, and in so doing retained the village's unique character, for which we should all be grateful.

Q. There are two churches on Montgomery Street. What is unusual about the one further up the hill?

Route:
Exiting Eaglesham leave by Gilmour Street retracing your steps, but just before the end of the village is a sign for Newton Mearns. Turn left at sign into the Humbie Road. Take 2nd. right at the roundabout, at the end of Humbie Road down Mearns Road. 200 metres on, turn left into Eaglesham Road and immediately on your left is a slip road leading to the next venue on the Eastwood District Route, which is Mearns Kirk.

MEARNS KIRK*

The story of Mearns Kirk begins in the 12th Century, when King David I returned from England inspired by what he had seen of the new Norman system of government and set about recreating it in his native land.

On the secular front this involved establishing a feudal system of land tenure, but a much more lasting change was to be in the religious sphere, with the division of the country into parishes, each under the effective control of a regional nobleman, who in turn owed his position to the King. In the case of Renfrewshire, this was the great Walter Fitzalan, who was to found the Stewart dynasty, and he it was who in 1163 founded the monastery in Paisley which was soon to become the Abbey that held sway over all the parishes of the county.

By 1190 the priest Helia de Perthic had arrived in this far flung corner of Renfrewshire to set up a church drawn, no doubt, by the castle built by Roland de Mearns and the dwellings that would have sprung up round it. Normally the church would have been sited close by, and together the three elements would have constituted a 'toun', but instead the priest chose a site a good distance away, giving credence to the theory that there had already been a Celtic church on this spot, dating from the 8th Century. Whatever, Helia's church was to survive for over six hundred years, among its more exotic connections one with the infamous Knights Templar, whom David 1 introduced into Scotland. There is in fact a gravestone in the churchyard bearing a sword and a cross, and legend has it that it marks the grave of one of these long dead crusaders.

Much later the Kirk saw its fair share of drama and tragedy during the times of the Covenanters, when the local congregation voted with their feet, rejecting successive Episcopalian curates who were foisted upon them. Not even a company of dragoons billeted in the nearby castle could prevent the Conventicles taking place, as the congregation moved out on to the nearby moorland. But as a result of neglect, the fabric of the church did suffer during this period, and it was only a matter of time before a new building became a necessity. Thus the present Kirk, which dates from 1813, and featured one great improvement on its predecessor... Seats! Yes, for the previous six centuries the congregation had remained standing.

Q. According to the notice board, on what date was the church founded?

Route:
Exiting Mearns Kirk turn right into Eaglesham Road then immediately right into Mearns Road. Go straight on (2nd exit) at roundabout, following signpost for Kilmarnock (A77). Just over 2 miles later this road merges with the A77, but just before, on the right hand side, is the next venue on the Eastwood District Route, the Robert Pollok Monument.

ROBERT POLLOCK MONUMENT

Robert Pollock was born in Eaglesham in 1798, the son of a farmer whose mother gave him the rudiments of an education at home until the age of eight, when he began to attend Mearns Parish School. He was obviously a gifted pupil for, at the age of fifteen, he transferred to Fenwick School to prepare for the College of Glasgow, as the University was then known. 1817 saw him pass through the portals of the famous old building on Glasgow's High Street, and over the next four years he was to study Latin and Greek, then latterly Moral Philosophy. By 1820 he had passed the examination to gain admission to the Divinity Hall of the United Seccession Church, but it was to be 1827 before he was licensed to preach the Gospel.

By this time he had already begun writing, initially with 'Tales of the Covenanters', inspired perhaps by the famous memorial to two of their number which graces Eaglesham's old cemetery. In fact the three tales, 'Helen of the Glen', 'Ralph Gemmel' and 'The Persecuted Family' were published anonymously, and not till after his death was his authorship acknowledged, as they could easily have left him open to persecution. What did make his name however was 'The Course of Time'. Stretching to an incredible 3500 verses this was Pollok's finest work, his examination of man's spiritual life, and the original manuscript now rests in the College Museum, Belfast.

But as with many artists, Pollok's life was to be tragically short, and if consumption sounds like a fitting end for a poet, the reality of tuberculosis in a Scottish Winter would have been anything but romantic. Having set out for Italy with his sister he could go no further than Southampton, where he died on 18th September 1827, at the age of 28. Buried at Millbrook, the inscription on his grave simply states, 'His immortal poem is his monument.' That proved to be the case in the years that followed, as 'The Course of Time' had reached its twenty fifth edition by 1867 , and his continuing fame was symbolised in the monument at Loganswell which was unveiled in 1900.

Its inscription is truly fitting. 'He soared untrodden heights and seemed at home.'

Q. On the monument, what is the poet holding in his hand?

Route:
Leaving the monument, turn sharp right on to the A77. After two miles you will come to a major junction, with a signpost for Barrhead. Turn left at the traffic lights into Barrhead Road then take second right behind a shopping centre into Capelrig Road. After one mile you will see a signpost pointing right to a road into Eastwood High school grounds. The signpost is for the next venue on the Eastwood District Route, which is Capelrig House.

CAPELRIG HOUSE

Following the Norman barons into the rich pickings of Renfrewshire in the 12th century came a powerful religious order of Crusaders. Formed to protect pilgrims in the Holy Lands, and undeterred by the comparative lack of Saracens in Newton Mearns, the Knights Templar set up business in what is now Capelrig.

The name originally meant chapel on the ridge, betraying its religious past, but as we know from the huge tenth century Celtic Cross found on the land, it is likely that this had long been holy ground. (More of this later.) As it was, the Templars' tenancy was to end early in the 14th century when the order was suppressed amidst accusations of sorcery and devil worship and the more acceptable order of Hospitallers took over. Then with the Reformation comes one of those fancy pieces of footwork for which our landed gentry are rightly famous, as the Preceptor of the order, Sir James Sandilands, 'embraced the reformed religion', and was created Lord Torphicen by an appreciative Queen

Mary. Thus did the lands fall into the hands of the Torphicen family.

By 1596 Capelrig had been acquired by the Mures of Caldwell, some of whom were detained during the time of the Covenanters, and for a while the estate was actually confiscated and handed over to Sir Thomas Dalziel, Commander of the Renfrewshire Persecutors. (A shovel was called a shovel in those days). Finally restored to the family in 1688, the house remained with the Mures until the 1700s, when the estate was sold to a Glasgow lawyer called Robert Barclay. It was he who in 1769 erected the house which stands there to the present day.

Anticipating something of Robert Adam's design at Archerfield in East Lothian, the projecting entrance bay lends grandeur to what is actually a modest-sized house, and with its balustrade and railwalk crowned with globes and matching vases, it was eventually designated an A-listed building which saved it from demolition in the 1960s. Today it is administered by the District Council for use as a cultural and recreational venue.

And the Celtic cross? Well it was moved to Kelvingrove Art Galleries in the 1920s, but legend has it that it made up one point of a triangle in the middle of which was a treasure fit for a king. The second point is reputed to be in the middle of the Gorbals Water Works but, sad to say, no-one knows the third! Perhaps the farmer who dug up a bronze age hammer in a nearby field in 1887 knew more than he let on!

Q. How many steps are there up to the front door?

Route:
Exiting Capelrig House, turn right into Capelrig Road and follow road to T-junction. Now turn right into Stewarton Road. At roundabout turn right, (3rd exit), signposted East Kilbride. This is Rouken Glen Road and 200 metres along to the right is a signpost for Rouken Glen Park, where you will find the penultimate venue on the Eastwood District Route, which is the Butterfly Kingdom.

ROUKEN GLEN
BUTTERFLY KINGDOM

What, you might ask yourself, and very understandably so, is a butterfly kingdom?

Well, imagine a giant greenhouse laid out like some strange botanic garden...the first thing that hits you is the humidity, air thick with the sweet smell of orange trees, bougainvillea and passion flowers, alive with the sound of birdsong and the teasing trickle of running water. All around, thousands of fluttering scraps of incandescent colour dance and spiral, kissing the petals and each other, as you follow a winding path across rustic wooden bridges, over a sudden waterfall that feeds the gushing streams which wind and twist their way between the wild tangle of foliage...
You get the idea..
Actually, this was the idea of Mr. Azam, proprietor of the Rouken Glen Garden Centre which adjoins the Kingdom of Butterflies. In creating a

balanced habitat for these tropical butterflies he has had to reproduce the conditions of an equatorial rainforest, with an average temperature of 80 degrees Fahrenheit, and to provide a wide range of exotic plants supplying the nectar on which they thrive. Most of the butterflies flying freely around you are actually breeding, so that the different stages of the life cycle are constantly enfolding... from egg to caterpillar, chrysalis to butterfly... before your very eyes.

There are also tropical birds, and an Insect Kingdom housing beetles and scorpions, stick insects and even tarantulas, though the arachnophobic amongst you will be happy to hear that unlike their winged cousins, these little chaps are kept safely behind glass!

Open 24th March - 7th Nov. Daily from 10.00 am - 5.00 pm.
Adults £1.95, children £1.00, (under 4 and disabled free).

Q. What colours is the butterfly on the sign above the door?

Route:
The Butterfly Kingdom is situated in Rouken Glen Park, which is also the last venue on the Eastwood District Route.

Rouken Glen

As a rule you won't find many wild Scottish glens complete with cliffs and waterfalls close to a major city, but where there's a rule there's always an exception to prove it, and Rouken Glen is just that.

The origin of the name is in doubt. Was it Rook End or Rock End? One school of thought is supported by the mention of a 'Rokandmyll' as far back as 1530, during the reign of James V, but there is the awkward and enduring fact that rooks do nest in the glen, and their screaming can be heard constantly, echoing among the crags. Suffice to say that Rouken was originally miller's lands near the falls, and the remains of the last mill are still visible in the rusting hub of the mill wheel.

The glen itself follows the line of the Auldhouse Burn which travels from Pilmuir and ends in the Cart at Pollockshaws, and was once the estate of two cotton merchants, John and Fred Pairman. They sold the house and lands to the ubiquitous calico printing magnate Walter Crum in 1858, and throughout the next half century, Thornliebank's first family lorded over the glen. Visitors to Birkenshaw House, (named after a local farm) included Lord Kelvin, the famous physicist, and a young Madeline Smith of Blythswood Square poisoning fame. Finally in 1905 it was bought by the future Lord Rowallan, who gifted it to the City of Glasgow the following year. Their plans to turn it into a zoo faltered after the First World War and the estate became what it is today....a public park.

Now run by Eastwood District Council, Rouken Glen somehow manages to retain its wildness within the confines of a public recreational facility. Grass, trees and a pond suddenly give way to the crags and cliffs of a Highland Glen, and the roar of water all but drowns out the screams of the swooping rooks who have been here since time immemorial.

Q. What is the name of the biennial arts festival which takes place in Rouken Glen?

Congratulations you have now completed the Eastwood District Route. If you wish to claim your free certificate signed by the Provost, proving that you have indeed Been & Seen Eastwood District, please cut out and send the coupon on page 24.

Route: (Returning to starting point)
Exiting Rouken Glen turn left into Rouken Glen Road, proceed to roundabout, drive right round the roundabout and return along Rouken Glen Road. Eastwood Park is on the left just before the next major roundabout.

Write your Eastwood District answers here:

Eastwood House:...

Thornliebank Library:...

White Cart Walkway:..

Greenbank House & Garden:..

Mearns Castle:..

Eaglesham:..

Mearns Kirk:..

Robert Pollock Monument:...

Capelrig House:...

Rouken Glen Butterfly Kingdom:..

Rouken Glen:..

To claim your free certificate proving that you have indeed Been and Seen the District of Eastwood, please complete the coupon below answering all the questions, cut along the dotted line and send it in an envelope to:

Tourism Executive
Renfrewshire Enterprise
27 Causeyside Street
Paisley
PA1 1UL

I have visited all eleven venues on the Eastwood District Route.
Signed..
Witnessed by..
PLEASE PRINT DETAILS BELOW CLEARLY IN BLACK INK
Name...Age......
Address...
....
....
Postcode........................ Country..................................
Which venue did you best like..
Which venue did you least like...
During your visit where did you stay overnight: (please tick)
Home ..... Friends/ Relatives ..... Bed & Breakfast ..... Camping ....
Hotel ..... Caravan ..... Youth Hostel ..... Self catering ..... Other ....
What is the main purpose of your visit to Eastwood District?
Part of a holiday, weekend or short break ..... Conference .....
On business: staying overnight ..... daytrip .....
Visiting friends / relatives ..... On a day trip or short visit from
home ..... To take part in the Eastwood District Route .....
Overall how would you rate the venues? much better than you
expected ..... a bit better than expected ..... much as expected .....
a bit disappointing ..... very disappointing .....
Did you feel welcome in Eastwood District? Yes ..... No .....
Would you visit Eastwood District again? Yes..... No.....
Would you recommend Eastwood District to friends?Yes..... No ....
What in your opinion is Eastwood District's best asset?..................
....
Please describe Eastwood District in one word...........................
Thank you for taking the time to answer the questions.

Eastwood District Route Overview

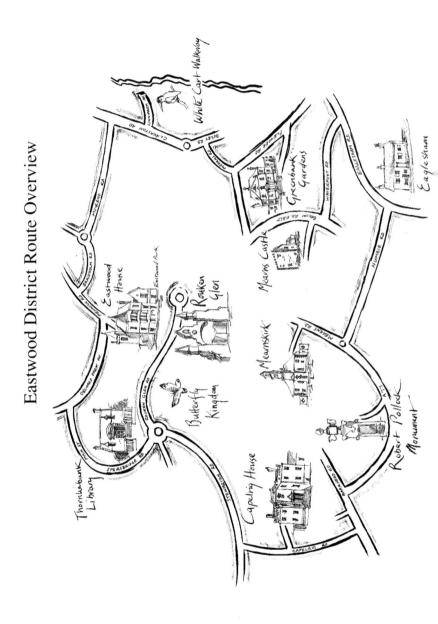

The venues marked with an * in the Eastwood District section are now available as signed, limited edition prints. If you wish to order please complete and send the coupon below to:

Been & Seen Publishing
PO Box 821 Gourock
Renfrewshire PA19 1LP
Scotland

Name..

Address..

....

....

Postcode....................Phone Number...

Please tick the print / s you wish to order

Please send me the following signed limited print / s:

Greenbank House	....
Eastwood House	....
Mearns Kirk	....
Wishing Well Tearooms	....

The size of each print is 296 x 420 mm. The cost of each print is £7.95. There is a limit of 850 signed numbered copies of each and orders will be dispatched on a strictly first come first served basis.. Each print is signed and numbered by the award winning artist Peter A. Michael. Please add £0.95 for packaging and delivery per order.UK only Please add £2.60 for packaging and delivery per order overseas. The above price of £7.95 includes VAT at 17.5%. Cheques payable to Been & Seen Publishing or alternatively please debit my credit card.

Access / Visa card number _ _ _ _ _ _ _ _ _ _ _ _ _ _ _ _

Expiry date _ _ / _ _ Signature_ _ _ _ _ _ _ _ _ _ _ _ _ _ _ _ _

Please allow 21 days for order processing and delivery.

For over 150 years people have been coming to the Inverclyde area for day trips. As Provost of Inverclyde, I am delighted to welcome you.

Last century visitors travelled here by steam boat or train to Port Glasgow, Greenock and Gourock, but today the choice is greater with the M8 motorway running to our boundary and Glasgow Airport only minutes away. Been & Seen Renfrewshire is designed for people with their own transport and in addition to the twelve venues described, you will discover that the towns and villages in Inverclyde boast some of the best scenery in the West of Scotland - as you will see when you visit the Lyle Hill and look across the river Clyde to the Argyll hills.

The 700 berth Marina at Inverkip and the large number of yachts racing off Gourock on summer evenings are proof that yachtsmen find sailing in the Clyde hard to beat.

I hope that you enjoy exploring Inverclyde and that you will return to see our other attractions which have not been included in this book.

Provost Allan Robertson
Inverclyde District Council

MUNICIPAL BUILDINGS GREENOCK*

A town hall says a great deal about a community, reflecting as it does not only its values and aspirations but the financial realities involved at the time of construction. In Greenock's case the search for grandeur was to meet head on with blatant greed.

The 1870s were a good time for Greenock and, as business boomed, so the need to replace the old Town Hall became ever more pressing. What was required was a building that would reflect the town's growing status, and be large enough to house all the departments of local government, such as police, fire, sanitary and cleansing. Eighty architects submitted proposals for the new Municipal Buildings, the successful candidate being Messrs. H&D Barclay of Glasgow, and the foundation stone was duly laid by Provost Dugald Campbell on 6th August, 1881, with attendant fireworks display and a banquet for 500.

This lavish start was typical of the extravagance that the Civic Authorities indulged in and speaking seven years later at a meeting concerning the insolvency of the Harbour Trust, a shipowner named Crawford stated that the construction of the buildings had 'involved every beauty but that of economy', and suggested that the offices of the Harbour Engineer could easily have been used as a first class hotel!

There was, however, one part of the building which did not rise to this high standard, for at what became known as Cowan's Corner, stately sandstone suddenly gave way to bare bricks. Cowan owned the piece of land at one corner of the new building but refused to sell holding out in the belief that the Council would finally meet his exorbitant price. But the guardians of the public purse had gone so far over budget that there was nothing left for the greedy chap, and the corner was still unrendered when it was hit by a German bomb in World War II, thus putting the matter to rest in dramatic fashion.

Cowan's Corner is now in fact a little garden for the blind, which seems rather apposite, considering its unlikely benefactor's lack of vision.

Open 8.30 am - 4.45 pm Mon-Fri. Information and Advice Centre also open these hours, and 9.30 am-12.30 pm Saturdays.

Q. Which part of a ship is being pulled by the three figures in Clyde Square?

Route:
Exiting Information and Advice Centre turn left along Clyde Square into Cathcart Street. Then at T junction turn left onto main road, take immediate first right across dual carriageway and 50 metres ahead you will see the next venue on the Inverclyde District Route, the Greenock Custom House.

GREENOCK CUSTOM HOUSE

When it comes to collecting excise duty it would seem that there have been more than a few colourful characters on both sides of the contraband fence as a visit to Greenock's Custom House Museum will soon reveal.

In 1816 a feu charter in perpetuity was issued to the commissioners in Edinburgh by the Burgh magistrates, but it was another eight years before the Custom House was complete, built at a cost of £30,000 with a labour force drawn mainly from veterans of the Napoleonic Wars. Perfectly placed at the Firth of Clyde, and already one of the leading British seaports, with a huge trade to all points West, including the West Indies and the eastern seaboard of America, Greenock now quickly became the principal customs port of the Clyde.

As such, the inhabitants of this fine waterfront building had not only the duty of filling the King's chest with silver for the Royal Mint, but preventing those scoundrels among the seafaring community who might perchance avoid paying their share. Today the chest and the smugglers' tools are all exhibits in a Museum which seeks to entertain as well as

inform. Here you can see what the well dressed 1840s exciseman wore, and get some flavour of his modern counterpart's lot by playing a computer game which involves searching a ship for drugs. Not that narcotics are the most exotic of the items that didn't get away... among the list of confiscated items are the skins of a leopard, an elephant and a crocodile, as well as a pair of cobra skin shoes!

Among the titbits of information you will pick up is that the King's mistress, Nell Gwynne, was once maintained from excise yield, (£6000 per annum), while famous personages who have worn the customs uniform include Chaucer, Daniel Defoe and the great Scottish economist, Adam Smith. But surely the most famous holder of the office has to be Rabbie Burns, who immortalised the sinecure in his poem, 'The deil's awa' wi' th' Exciseman'. No doubt the proud race of Highlanders who once distilled their own wee drap of the hard stuff wish he was!

Open Mon- Fri 10 am-12.30 pm, & 1.30-4.00 pm.

Q. What is at the top of the quaint clock tower in front of the Customs House?

Route:
Leave Custom House and turn left on to the A8, signposted Port Glasgow. Continue into Port Glasgow with the giant Scott Lithgow crane on your left hand side till you see a sign for the Town Centre pointing right. Turn right into Shore Street which snakes to the left, and across the carpark to your left you will see the next venue on the Inverclyde District Route, which is the Comet Replica.

THE COMET REPLICA

Sitting proudly across from Port Glasgow town centre you will find the magnificent replica of Henry Bell's Comet, resplendent in original maroon and black, its bow picked out in white, commissioned in 1962 to celebrate the launching of the original 150 years before.

Although the name 'Comet' will forever be synonymous with the birth of steam travel, the story might have been rather different if another Scotsman by the name of William Symington had succeeded in persuading the owners of the Forth and Clyde Canal that steamboats would not damage their precious waterways. As early as 1802 this parson turned civil engineer had launched the Charlotte Dundas on the canal, and not only had it sailed under its own steam, it had towed other vessels as well, but when his backer, the Duke of Bridgewater, died suddenly, Symington threw in the towel.

Then with one of those vicious quirks of fate that twist the dagger in a man already down, one of Symington's guests on board the maiden voyage of the Charlotte Dundas went on to build the world's first commercial steamship. An American by the name of Fulton, he actually offered Napoleon the chance to convey his troops across the Channel by steamships for the invasion of England, but having been politely turned down, he returned to America and in 1807 began a service on the Hudson that plied between New York and Albany.

So it was left to Henry Bell, who had been grappling with the problem for years, to produce the first commercially viable steamboat in Europe. Fittingly she was to ply her trade on the Clyde, having rolled off the stocks of John Wood's Port Glasgow in January of 1812, all forty feet in length, and ten foot six inches beam. Fitted with sails, her three horse power engine drove four paddle-wheels, two on either side, and she ran regularly between Glasgow, Greenock and Helensburgh, so initiating the ritual that was to enter the couthy Glaswegian vocabulary as 'goin doon the watter'.

Unfortunately her replica has only a shallow pond to sit in, but even with this constraint it is easy to imagine the furore that the original Comet must have caused on the waters of the Clyde all those years ago.

Q. What colour is the Comet's hull?

Route:
Exit car park and turn left along Shore Street and as you turn the bend, you will see directly ahead of you the old Port Glasgow Town Building, which is the next venue on the Inverclyde District Route.

PORT GLASGOW
TOWN BUILDING

As if mirroring the receding tide of commerce and industry which once swelled the coffers of the towns along the Clyde, Port Glasgow's Town Building now sits much further from the great wealth-giving river than was once the case.

For centuries Irvine, on the Ayrshire coast, had been Glasgow's accepted port but as trade blossomed in the 17th century so the need for a deep water harbour on the Clyde grew. Already spurned in their search by both

Dumbarton and Troon then baulked by Greenock, Glasgow's merchants finally turned their attention in 1668 to Sir Patrick Maxwell's Newark estate on the river west of Langbank. Presented with an offer of 1300 merks, (£72.20), and sensing the impending wind of change, the Laird showing the type of foresight not always associated with the Scottish gentry, took the money and ran.

At first named Newport Glasgow, the town grew quickly in stature and by 1762 had the first graving dock in Scotland, with pumps courtesy of James Watt. True, the deepening further upriver would gradually affect Port Glasgow's general trade, but by the end of the century it was specialising in timber, and with some seven hundred ships using its docks annually, its future looked assured. It was in this climate that the famous Glasgow architect David Hamilton was commissioned to design a town building to sit beside the harbour, and the elegant result with its Doric portico and 180 foot high steeple reflects the high point of the town's history.

In those days the municipal building was expected to house the whole shooting match, in this case the administrative offices, commercial counting houses, a large reading room, the law court and police station. This last mentioned had its entrance round at the side, right at the harbour edge, and the story goes that one morning a discharged drunk staggered out of the door, tripped headlong into the Clyde and drowned! So if it was that close to the water, I hear you ask, how come it's a few hundred yards away now? Well the fact is that the harbour was filled in before World War II.

In the meantime the town had built, demolished and rebuilt yet another municipal headquarters, leaving Anderson's fine building to face the ravages of time. But against all the odds it has hung on, and having survived the ravages of the 1960s, its future seems at last secure.

Q. What is unusual about the six foot weather vane?
Route:
Leaving the Port Glasgow Town Building, turn right into Fore Street, then right again at the traffic lights back on to the A8. Follow road to first roundabout, and take left (1st exit) signposted Newark Castle, which is the next venue on the Inverclyde District Route.

NEWARK CASTLE

The single most important factor in Newark Castle's long history must surely be its unfortunate location. Built in the 15th Century on what would have been a lonely promontory on the banks of the Clyde, with magnificent panoramic views of the Firth, the estate which once surrounded it eventually fell victim to the long arm of commerce reaching 'doon the watter' from the growing metropolis of Glasgow.

The original owners of the castle were the Maxwell family and it was in the late 16th Century that Patrick Maxwell built the fine turreted mansion that connects the earlier tower and gatehouse, leaving his monogram all over the stonework in the process. His inscription above the door desired that the 'blissings of God be herein', but from 1694 this pious hope would only have benefited tenants, for after that date the castle was never inhabited by its owners. This may well be due to the fact that 18 acres of the estate had been sold to Glasgow's civic authorities in 1668 and the once secluded castle was soon cheek by jowl with the burgeoning port and harbour which was to become Port Glasgow. Once begun, the march of 'progress' was unstoppable, and by 1800 the castle was surrounded by shipyards, churning out tall masted sailing ships at a fair rate of knots.

Nowadays the high tide of shipbuilding has long receded and the industrial flotsam and jetsam which it left behind has finally been cleared, revealing Newark Castle in something resembling its original setting. The shore line has been reinforced and the old pier has been renovated, while the area around the castle has been imaginatively landscaped with a network of footpaths giving access to its grounds, now named Newark Castle Park.

Open April - September 9.30 am - 6.30 pm, Sundays 2.00 - 6.30 pm.
October - March 9.30 am - 4.00 pm, Sundays 2.00 - 6.30 pm.
There is a charge for admission.

Q. What initials make up the monograms above the windows?

Route:
Exiting Newark Castle turn left back on to the A8 and follow dual carriageway straight through next roundabout signposted Glasgow. Shortly after the reduce speed sign you will see the signpost on the other side of the dual carriageway for Finlaystone House. Turn right across the carriageway into the drive of Finlaystone House, which is the next venue on the Inverclyde District Route.

FINLAYSTONE HOUSE*

Any country house worth its salt should have a wealth of stories, and Finlaystone House, overlooking the Clyde near Langbank, is certainly no exception. Originally the home of the Cunninghams, who begat fifteen Earls of Glencairn, the house dates from the 14th century and was to remain in their family for over five hundred years. It was in the garden, with its magnificent views across the Clyde estuary, that John Knox gave Communion under a yew tree in 1556, to the assembled household of Alexander, the 5th Earl. An outspoken supporter of the Reformation, he was also known as the Good Earl, (a title which does tend to pose questions of his predecessors), and though he and his eminent visitor have long passed into history, the tree in question is still standing on the West side of the house, though not in its original setting, having been moved in 1900 when Finlaystone underwent extensive restyling.

Two centuries later another famous (if slightly less reputable) visitor was to grace Finlaystone, this time in the shape of Robert Burns. In fact it is arguable that without this connection, Scotland might never have had its national bard, for according to Burns himself, he was rescued from wretchedness and exile by James Cunningham, the 14th Earl of Glencairn, who was to become his first patron. So grateful was Rabbie that he called his son James Glencairn and there does seem to have been a genuine bond of affection between them for, on the Earl's untimely death in 1791, Burns wrote the following:

> 'The mother may forget the child
> That smiles sae sweetly on her knee,
> But I'll remember thee, Glencairn
> And a' that thou has done for me!'

Not one of his best, perhaps, but obviously heartfelt.

Nowadays Finlaystone is the home of the Clan MacMillan, and its grounds have become a Country Park with walks through wild woodland replete with waterfalls and picnic areas. The complex also boasts a shop and a small gallery of Celtic exhibits, together with a secluded walled garden, while in Summer its formal gardens are alive with colour and are rightly famed for the variety of plants and exotic flowers.

peter Machael '93

Q. What is the name of Finlaystone's shop?

Route:
Leave Finlaystone by the rear driveway, and as you exit right, cross the road and turn left immediately into a narrow country road which will take you to Kilmacolm. As you enter Kilmacolm by Finlaystone Road this will become Market Place, continue to T-junction at Port Glasgow Road. Turn left into Bridge of Weir Road and about a mile further on follow the signpost to the right for Quarriers Village continue down this road and over the bridge, turn left at the T-junction and left again into Craigend Avenue. You are now in Quarriers Village which is the next venue on the Inverclyde District Route.

QUARRIER'S VILLAGE, BRIDGE OF WEIR

If any one word could hope to explain why a self made businessman should devote his life to saving orphans from the horrors of deprivation in Victorian Glasgow, that word must be 'conscience'.

Born in Greenock in 1829, William Quarrier lost his father at the age of three, and faced with the prospect of the dreaded Poor House, his widowed mother moved her small family to Glasgow, where she eked a frugal living taking in fine sewing. Years later the small boy remembers standing shoeless in the rain on High Street, watching the better off go by, oblivious to the grinding poverty around them, and in that moment is crystallised the conviction that if ever he finds himself in their shoes, he will not walk on by.

At the age of six he is working twelve hours a day fitting heads to hatpins for one shilling a week. By seven he is apprenticed to a shoemaker in Paisley and by twelve he is a time served journeyman. At seventeen he is employed by a devout Baptist called Mrs. Hunter who invites him to her Church where he undergoes a conversion. Ten years later he will marry her daughter, but by then he will be in business for himself, soon to become one of the first multiple shoe shop owners in Glasgow. And then one night on his way home he sees a child matchstick seller weeping on the street, his stock stolen, hunger beckoning, and he remembers the promise that the shoeless boy made all those years ago.

In the next five years he sets up a shoeblack brigade in the city, giving the boys a uniform, brushes and blacking and two thirds of their earnings... then a newsboy brigade and a parcel brigade, all of this leading to a mission which sends more than 6000 children to a new life in Canada. From thence to forty acres of farmland near the Bridge of Weir, (price £3560), and within ten years the waters of the Gryffe are flowing through a village of over forty sandstone cottages complete with its own church, school, shop and tradesmen.

At its zenith in the 1920s, the village held almost 1600 children, but after the war came the Welfare State, and with it legislation that would slowly change the conditions which had made Quarrier's so necessary. By the 1960s each house held only eight children, deemed to be the magic ratio by experts in the caring field, but that formula too was swept away by social change. Nowadays more than half the houses are privately owned, while others cater for adults with learning needs and the elderly in a multi discipline caring environment. So while other institutions have sent their residents out into the community, Quarriers have reversed the process by bringing the community in.

And William Quarrier? Well he lies in the quiet graveyard behind the Gothic Church, whose melodic bells have rung out the quarters across the quiet Renfrewshire countryside for over a hundred years.

Q. What was the name of the house in which William Quarrier lived on Faith Avenue?

Route:

Exiting Faith Avenue turn right, leaving village past Hattrick Farm. At T-junction turn right onto the B786 for Kilmacolm. Follow road until you see the B788 signposted Greenock, then turn left. At the top of the climb you will pass a large electricity generating station, then as you come down into the outskirts of Greenock turn left at the T-junction, and left again at the traffic lights into Drumfrochar Road, signposted Largs. As you reach Overton Primary School on your right, take a left turn into the Old Largs Road. Continue with the golf course to your left then along single track road across moorland, and Loch Thom will appear on your right hand side. Follow road round the Loch till you reach a signpost for Inverkip and Cornalees to the right. Turn right and follow the road to the next venue on the Inverclyde District Route, which is Cornalees.

CORNALEES

If you fancy a marvellous country walk without getting your boots too dirty, then I suggest you try the nature trail at Cornalees.

Sitting above the Clyde estuary on the banks of Loch Thom, at the edge of the moors, Cornalees is the western tip of 102 square miles of wonderfully varied countryside that make up the magnificent Clyde Muirshiel Regional Park. Muirshiel is actually a complex of individual country parks, each with its own distinctive identity and its own fauna and flora and in the case of Cornalees this means the loch and its trout fishing, together with a series of walks that bring you directly into contact with the surrounding countryside.

The well sign posted nature trail will take you down Shielhill Glen, above a delightfully meandering stream which has cut deep into the hillside, then suddenly the path begins to drop and you find yourself in another world, a tiny valley full of leafy ferns dappled with broken sunlight, the air still save for the buzz of insects, the gently rippling water trickling white over the time-smoothed rocks. Now the trail begins to criss cross the stream, and you stand for a long moment looking down at the quiet dark eddies beneath the bridge, drinking in the peace. Here, at the bottom of the small ravine, the path becomes a twisting snake, then you are aware that the boardwalk path before you is beginning to rise, a few moments later you are out of the trees at the edge of the moorland, squat heather glinting its pinks and purples and, as you climb, the panorama of the Argyll hills opens up above the silver sweep of Lunderston Bay.

Along the trail you will find benches which have been dedicated to loved ones and after the climb you may feel the need to sit and rest awhile. If you still have the energy you can tackle the walk along the Greenock Cut, an aqueduct which took water down to the thirsty mills, but there again, you may just want to sit back and enjoy one of the best views in Scotland. So go on, treat yourself!

Q.What is the name of the trout fishery situated beside the car park?

Route:
Exiting Cornalees turn right down road which runs right through Shielhill Farm. Take a left at the T-junction for Inverkip. As you reach a modern estate, the road becomes a chicane. So turn left into Swallow Brae, and immediately right down Millhouse Road. Turn right at the T- junction, and 100 metres ahead turn right into Inverkip Main Street. At the end of Main Street you meet the main A78 road. Turn right heading for Greenock till you see the signpost for the A770 to Gourock. Turn left and follow this road till you reach the next venue on the Inverclyde District Route, the Cloch Lighthouse.

CLOCH LIGHTHOUSE*

The waters of the Firth of Clyde can be treacherous at the best of times, and as the locals of this part of the world will tell you, weatherwise the best of times are relatively few and far between. Hence the Clyde's three lighthouses.

The first, built in 1757, was the Cumbrae lighthouse whose Trustees were empowered to collect between one halfpenny and twopence per ton of cargo from the ships which came up and down the river. The shipowners paying these dues were predominately Glasgow merchants, and as they watched the operating surplus gradually rise, they put increasing pressure on the Trustees for more light on the river. The obvious place was at Cloch Point, the narrowest point of the estuary between Renfrewshire and Cowal where ferries had plied from as far back as the 6th century kingdom of Dalriada, but the narrowness of the straits had proved a continual threat to shipping over the years.
Eventually built in 1796 by the firm of Kermack and Gall, and using a six wick lamp to produce 2000 candle power, the lighthouse was first

manned by Alan McLean, a Greenock pilot, who received the princely sum of £30 per annum. Glasgow architect, James Clarkson, produced a design which saw the broad tower rise 80 feet to a wallhead walk above which the facetted dome beams its light across the Firth. After 1903 that light was produced by acetylene gas which upped the power by a factor of ten, and at the same time a new revolving apparatus was fitted which created a flash every five seconds with a visibility reckoned to be nineteen miles.

Around the turn of the century the Cloch was in hot water with the locals after a fog horn was fitted, but whether due to complaints or lack of success, the experiment was discontinued. During both Wars a boom was strung between Cloch and Dunoon to deter enemy submarines, and a gun emplacement was built just along the shore. But as it headed towards its bi-centenary, its lighthouse keepers fell victim to technology, and since 1973 the Cloch has been unmanned, its living quarters now divided into three private houses, boasting one of the best views in the country.

Q. What is the emblem on the black shield above the front door?

Route:
Leaving Cloch Lighthouse continue along the A770 through Gourock. The main road will become Eldon Street, then with Battery Park on your left, turn right into Lyle Road at the British Rail sign. Continue through crossroads under a railway bridge signposted to Lyle Hill, climbing and snaking until you reach a give way sign. Take a sharp left, and up ahead you will see the Cross of Lorraine which is at the brow of Lyle Hill, the next venue on the Inverclyde District Route.

Lyle Hill

In times of high unemployment, the idea of job creation usually rears its head in some guise or other, and so it was at the end of the 19th Century when Greenock's Provost, Abraham Lyle, came up with a job creation scheme which would not only make a stunning view of the Clyde Estuary more accessible to the citizens of the town, but gain him a little slice of immortality into the bargain.

Lyle's project involved creating a road over the then un-named hill which rears up behind the tenements of Greenock on one side and the picturesque Cardwell Bay on the other, and on its summit constructing a lookout point.

Now fine a job as those denizens of the dole definitely did, the real credit must go to the good Provost, for the panorama that awaits you on the crest of Lyle Hill is truly spectacular. Looking out over the broad expanse of the Firth of Clyde and Cardwell Bay, the view encompasses the Holy Loch, Gare Loch and Loch Long, sweeping from faraway Yetts Moor in the south to Ben Bowie in the north east and on a good day the highest peaks of Arran 45 miles away.

To help you put names to the main features, the AA has provided a Capstan, and so you can identify Cruach nam Miseag, Sligrachan Hill, Sgorach Mor and Beinn Bhreac... how wonderfully alive they sound in their Gaelic, these last survivors of what was once the predominant native culture. (After such poetry, the Cobbler at the head of Loch Long doesn't quite have the same ring.) But if you turn and follow the line of the Clyde towards the sprawl of the city and the haze that covers it, you will see the reason for the demise of a culture that had such poetry in its soul. Long after Provost Lyle had passed away, the good citizens of Greenock found another use for his promontory by siting the Free French Memorial here, as a tribute to the men who had been stationed in the town during the Second World War. Known as the Cross of Lorraine, it is hard to imagine a more impressive site for this modern reminder of the Auld Alliance.

Q. Name one of the Free French vessels which was sunk during
World War II?

Route:
Leave the Cross of Lorraine and descend Lyle Hill in the opposite
direction to the way you arrived. This becomes Newton Street. Continue
then turn left into Robertson Street immediately after Ardgowan Primary
School. Then take the fourth turning on the right, opposite the Tontine
Hotel. Continue along Union Street and just after the traffic lights you
will see, on your right, the next venue on the Inverclyde District Route,
the Watt Memorial Library.

WATT MEMORIAL LIBRARY

Unlike many great men with humble provincial origins James Watt maintained a lifelong connection with his birthplace and his long shadow is still evident in Greenock to this day. Witness his donation of £100 to the town magistrates in 1816 for the setting up of a scientific library whose subjects were to range from the art of shipbuilding to the properties of fluids, thus beginning a collection which was to form a vital part of what has become known as the Watt Memorial Library.

Greenock already had a Public Subscription Library as early as 1783, (making it the oldest in Scotland), and after Watt's death in 1819 his son offered to provide a building to house both collections. So it was that in 1837 Edward Blore's Northern English Tudor Style building opened, its classical pillars supporting a first floor gallery, its foyer dominated by a magnificent marble statue of Watt himself. This monument, which gives the library its name, had been commissioned by the good townspeople of

Greenock on their benefactor's death, and there it sits to this very day, as pristine white as the morning it left Sir Francis Chantrey's studio.

As well as housing Watt's scientific collection, the library itself is a mine of local information, with material on ships and shipbuilding, sugar refining and ropemaking, and historical archives on all things pertaining to Inverclyde. Its other main claim to fame, though, is of the literary sort, for it is here that the Burns 'Mother Club' has made its home. Founded in 1801 by a group of the Bard's admirers, including some who had known the great man himself, this august gathering held their first Supper on 29th January 1802. Little did they know what they were beginning, but it is to them that we owe the ritual which allows people of five continents to join in celebrating a ploughman's son, and thus to become honorary Scots, for one night each year.

Open Mon & Thurs 2 am - 5 pm, 6 pm - 8 pm. Wed & Sat 10 am - 1 pm.
Tues & Fri 10 am - 1 pm, 2 pm - 5 pm.
The Burns Room is open by arrangement with Club Representatives.

Q. Whose portrait is to the left inside the entranceway?

Route:
The next venue on the Inverclyde District Route is adjoining the library. So turn left and left again and you are at the door of the McLean Museum and Art Gallery.

Peter Nimmo '93

McLEAN MUSEUM
& ART GALLERY*

Named after, and founded by a local timber Merchant, Greenock's
McLean Museum and Art Gallery is a prime example of the maxim that
small can be beautiful.

Housed in a building which adjoins the Watt Monument Library, the
museum consists of an open ground floor and a first floor balcony
supported by tall metal pillars. The interior itself is spacious and
uncluttered, elegant cornice contrasting with ornate metalwork, providing an atmosphere marvelously redolent of those burgeoning late
Victorian days which spawned the wealth that built it. Greenock's
industries occupy the ground floor space, heavy exhibits that tell of
shipbuilding, both sail and the steam, as well as sugar refining and
ropemaking. James Watt's contribution is there, his achievements
towering over that of his fellow citizens, while yet another section
celebrates the Comet, though for intensity of purpose, the huge glass
cased harpoon takes some beating.

Upstairs is divided into sections, most of them geographical, but here the scale is suddenly more human, with a sailor's valentine lovingly arranged from a variety of coloured shells and a ship in a bottle. Stuffed animals are nothing new, but information on the sportsman is unusual in a museum setting, and so RL Scott's collection of trophies has an immediacy that other taxidermist's subjects normally lack. When you know that the magnificent crocodile was bagged on the Nile on a certain day at a certain time, and there's a photo of the kill to prove it, somehow it brings home the enormity of the culture change that 60 years has wrought in man's thinking. Suddenly Mr. Scott is the exhibit, not the crocodile.

The art collection boasts over 800 paintings, which are normally shown in rotation, and includes works by Courbet and Corot, as well as acknowledged classics by Scottish masters like Raeburn, Ramsay and Hornel.
Open Mon - Sat 10-12 & 1-5 pm.

Q. Whose portrait is to the left inside the entranceway?

Congratulations you have now completed the Inverclyde District Route. If you wish to claim your free certificate signed by the Provost, proving that you have indeed Been & Seen Inverclyde, please cut out and send the coupon on page 54.

Write your Inverclyde District answers here:

Municipal Buildings:...

Greenock Custom House:..

The Comet Replica:...

Port Glasgow Town Building:...

Newark Castle:...

Finlaystone House:..

Quarriers Village:..

Cornalees:...

Cloch Lighthouse:...

Lyle Hill:..

Watt Memorial Library:...

McLean Museum:...

To claim your free certificate proving that you have indeed Been and Seen the District of Inverclyde, please complete the coupon below answering all the questions, cut along the dotted line and send it in an envelope to:

Tourism Executive
Renfrewshire Enterprise
27 Causeyside Street
Paisley
PA1 1UL

I have visited all twelve venues on the Inverclyde District Route.
Signed..
Witnessed by..
PLEASE PRINT DETAILS BELOW CLEARLY IN BLACK INK
Name...Age......
Address...
....
....
Postcode...................... Country....................................
Which venue did you best like...
Which venue did you least like...
During your visit where did you stay overnight: (please tick)
Home ..... Friends/ Relatives ..... Bed & Breakfast ..... Camping ...
Hotel ..... Caravan ..... Youth Hostel ..... Self catering ..... Other ....
What is the main purpose of your visit to Inverclyde District?
Part of a holiday, weekend or short break ..... Conference .....
On business: staying overnight ..... daytrip .....
Visiting friends / relatives ..... On a day trip or short visit from
home ..... To take part in the Inverclyde District Route .....
Overall how would you rate the venues? much better than you
expected ..... a bit better than expected ..... much as expected .....
a bit disappointing ..... very disappointing .....
Did you feel welcome in Inverclyde? Yes ..... No .....
Would you visit Inverclyde again? Yes ..... No .....
Would you recommend Inverclyde to friends? Yes ..... No .....
What in your opinion is Inverclyde's best asset?......................
....
Please describe Inverclyde in one word................................
Thank you for taking the time to answer the questions.

Inverclyde District Route Overview

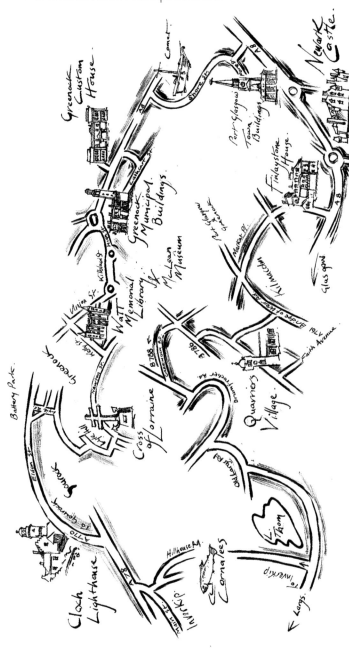

The venues marked with an * in the Inverclyde section are now available as signed, limited edition prints. If you wish to order please complete and send the coupon below to:

Been & Seen Publishing
PO Box 821 Gourock
Renfrewshire PA19 1LP
Scotland

Name..

Address..

....

....

Postcode....................Phone Number................................

Please tick the print / s you wish to order
Please send me the following framed limited edition signed print / s:

Cloch Lighthouse   ....
Greenock Municipal Buildings   ....
McLean Museum and Art Gallery   ....
Finlaystone House   ....

The size of each print is 296 x 420 mm. The cost of each print is £7.95. There is a limit of 850 signed numbered copies of each and orders will be dispatched on a strictly first come first served basis. Each print is signed and numbered by the award winning artist Peter A. Michael. Please add £0.95 for packaging and delivery per order. UK only. Please add £2.60 for packaging and delivery per order overseas. The above price of £7.95 includes VAT at 17.5%. Cheques payable to Been & Seen Publishing or alternatively please debit my credit card.

Access / Visa card number _ _ _ _ _ _ _ _ _ _ _ _ _ _ _ _

Expiry date _ _ / _ _ Signature _ _ _ _ _ _ _ _ _ _ _ _ _ _ _ _

Please allow 21 days for order processing and delivery.

As Provost of Renfrew District I am delighted to be involved in the production of Been & Seen Renfrewshire.

May I extend a very warm welcome to all our guests visiting the District. The twelve venues mentioned in this book are well worth a visit so please, take your time, relax and enjoy the scenery and visit our many places of interest en route.

Throughout the District there are many other attractions, for example the view from Gleniffer Braes in Paisley is superb and, for anyone interested in watersports, why not visit Castle Semple Water Park in Lochwinnoch. If you wish to spend some leisure time in and around Paisley, our top class Lagoon Leisure Centre is an ideal venue for adults and children alike and we boast one of the finest skating rinks in Scotland.

I do hope that you enjoy your stay with us and look forward to signing your certificate on completion of the Renfrew District Route.

Provost William. F. Orr
Renfrew District Council

The Paisley town section of the Renfrew District Route is best done on foot, so park your car in one of the town's car parks (the multi storey car park in Central Road just off Smithhills Street is nearest to the Town Hall, the first venue on the Route) and make your way to the Town Hall to start your exploration.

PAISLEY TOWN HALL

Paisley's name is synonymous with thread so it is only fitting that it should owe its town hall to the generosity of a man whose ancestors first developed cotton thread as a viable replacement to linen.

It was during the Napoleonic wars that the supply of silk from the Continent began to dry up and Paisley, already a prosperous weaving centre, soon began to feel the pinch. Necessity thus begat invention for brothers James and Patrick Clark who had a small business selling loom parts and the result, seemingly discovered by accident, was a strong durable cotton thread. By 1812 a factory was in full swing and the rest, as they say, is history. Both brothers had sons who were to continue the good work but it was James' son George who was to be the benefactor of the town hall leaving a legacy of £20,000 for the purpose.

Opened in 1882 with much accompanying fanfare, the building complied with Clark's will by being erected on the East side of the Cart, in the New Town where he was born. Witness of the benefactor's largesse

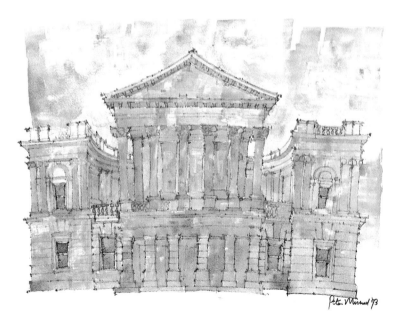

can be found at the entrance, in the family's anchor emblem emblazoned on the fine wrought iron gates and once through them, you find yourself in the foyer which now serves as the Paisley Tourist Information Centre - operated by Greater Glasgow Tourist Board. The interior of the building has recently been renovated, and though the foyer has been re-modelled, the hall itself looks much as it would have done on the January day it opened. With a capacity of nine hundred it is used for everything from book fairs to fiddlers' rallies, and if you want to get the best of the latter, the inside info is to sit at the back of the top gallery (unless of course you suffer from vertigo).

On leaving, check out the rear of the building with its asymmetrical towers, the larger of which houses four figures representing the seasons, and if your timing is correct you'll hear the gentle reassuring chimes of the bells in the clock tower pealing out across the river.

Open Mon - Sat 9am - 6 pm, later when events demand.

Q. There are two marble busts in the doorway. What is the date on the base of each?

Pedestrian route:
Exiting Paisley Town Hall, turn left up Abbey Close, left into Gauze Street, 2nd right into Moss Street first left into School Wynd, and branch right at church into Oakshaw Street East. Proceed up hill till you see on your left the next venue on the Renfrew District Route, which is the Coats Observatory.

COATS
OBSERVATORY

When the members of the Paisley Philosophical Institution gathered for their Annual Meeting in 1880, a proposition was made that an astronomical telescope be bought, and housed in the new Museum-Library Complex. The name of the gentleman who put forward the motion is long forgotten, but the member who responded to the call belonged predictably to Paisley's first family.

Thomas Coats, then a member of the council, not only offered to defray the cost of such a purchase but went one better and set about providing a building in which to house it. Such magnanimity has ensured that the name Coats lives on, this time attached to the Observatory. It was built on ground set aside for possible extensions to the Museum and opened for business in October 1883 though, sadly, Thomas Coats was prevented from opening it through ill health, and died two weeks later. The architect responsible, John Honeyman, had in fact incorporated ramps in his design to accommodate Mr. Coats' wheelchair, making the Observatory one of the first public buildings to attempt to cater for the disabled.

At the time of its opening Paisley had one of the best equipped small observatories in the country, with its 5 inch telescope by Cooke of York, a transit instrument, sidereal clocks and specialised eyepieces, and by 1898 these had been joined by a 10 inch telescope by Grubb of Dublin. Weather recording activities had been initiated in 1884, a process which has continued uninterrupted to the present day. The daily returns to the Meteorological Office include wind speed, rainfall and temperature and barometric pressure. Two seismic recorders were also installed in a specially constructed building and records include readings from the great San Francisco earthquake of 1906.

Activity dwindled in the 1920s as the value of the original endowment fell and after World War Two a financial crisis was only averted by the goodwill of the last curator who kept his salary at pre-war levels. Finally, on his retiral in 1957, the Philosophical Institution was forced to resort to a proviso in the original deed of gift that allowed the Observatory to be offered to Paisley Town Council, and after six years of negotiations it finally assumed control. After the local government reorganisation of 1975 it fell to Renfrew District Council to undertake extensive and much needed repairs to coincide with the centenary of the building. Now with the updating of equipment the Observatory receives pictures from weather satellites and has become the major seismic station in south west Scotland. So through good times and bad the Observatory has endured, although it might truly be said that Mr. Thomas Coats could never have imagined how 'farsighted' his generosity would turn out to be.

Open Mon, Tue, Thurs, 2-8 pm. Wed, Fri, Sat 10-5 pm.
Q. What is the date above the front door?

Pedestrian route:
Retrace your steps down Oakshaw Street East, and take the first lane to the right which turns to the right into Orr Square. At the bottom of the hill bear right along High Street till you reach the next venue on the Renfrew District Route, which is Paisley Museum and Art Galleries.

PAISLEY MUSEUM AND ART GALLERIES

Honeyman's impressive ionic portico promises a building on the grand Victorian scale, making it all the more refreshing to find such a classically simple interior as the setting for this museum.

The four enlarged photographs in the entrance hall set the tone; sharp atmospheric shots of late nineteenth century Paisley, so real you feel you could walk into them. The focus here is on the history of the ordinary person in the street, and the theme continues on the first floor balcony with more of the ephemera from everyday life. Among the displays is one on the temperance movement, with a photograph of the wonderfully named Teetotal Tower, a soft drinks temple built by a bookseller named George Caldwell.

All Paisley life is here, the mundane and the dramatic... everything from a giant meat pickling jar to the Death Warrant and Executioner's Contract of the burgh's last public hanging in January 1858. Industry has its place... shipbuilding on the Cart (in 1917 George V launched three boats from three separate yards in one hour) and of course the famous Paisley shawls. The ultimate accolade for any product is to acquire the generic name (like Hoover or Guinness or Biro) and the Paisley Pattern is one of that rare breed (though the credit for the design should go to 2000 year old Indo European cultures). In some ways this wonderful collection of shawls, with its richness of detail and depth of colour, embodies the reason for the Museum's existence, for it was Sir Peter Coats, yet another member of the ubiquitous thread family, who provided the building for the Paisley Philosophical Society to house its existing collections. Local interest aside, the museum also boasts the only pre-Reformation manuscript service books to survive in Scotland, and two silver bells from 1608 and 1620, among the world's oldest extant racing trophies, while the contemporary ceramics collection is regarded as second only in quality to the Victoria and Albert Museum in London. Add a splendid Natural History section and an Art Gallery with a collection of fine paintings which includes some 'classics' by artists of the Glasgow School and you have a most stimulating experience.

Open Mon - Sat 10 am - 5 pm.

Q. What is the subject of the museum's main collection?

Pedestrian route:
Exiting the Museum, turn right along High Street and you will shortly
reach the next venue on the Renfrew District Route, which is the Coats
Memorial Church.

COATS MEMORIAL CHURCH*

Churches of cathedral proportions are not normally dedicated to the memory of mere mortals, but there again, in Paisley the Coats family have never quite fallen into that category.

The date on the red notice board at the gate reads 1894, by which time Thomas Coats had been dead some eleven years, but in fact the idea of a memorial church for the famous thread magnate had been conceived within months of his death. Six architects had been invited to submit design proposals in the Gothic style, with a budget of £10,000, and projected seating for 800, but in keeping with the spirit of both age and project the winner was the magnificently monikered Hippolyte J Blanc who in due course was to deliver a building every bit as Gothic as his name at a cost of £110,000. (Hence, of course, the ten year delay).

But the wait was well worthwhile, from the tip of the teeth on the facade's splendid gargoyles to the almost invisible intricacies of carving in the barrel vaulted ceiling, Hippolyte's church is an extended essay of loving detail. Given his head, the architect embraced this opportunity of a lifetime to make up for all the shoddy compromises normally demanded of that most maligned of professions. From the first step into the foyer, with its magnificent Byzantine tesserae comprising 350,000 separate pieces of coloured marble, to the stunning angel and scripture adorned roof of the chancel, no expense has been considered let alone spared. Given the time and the means Blanc succeeded in creating a wonderful memorial not only to Thomas Coats, but also to the craftsmen of his day.

Their work is there at every turn; on the pew ends, each with its own unique carving, on the bronze eagle which supports the Bible on the lectern, in the mosaic of the chancel floor, and in the oak and gilded brass of the rostrum. In a range of delights there are even higher peaks; with the white marble pulpit and its alabaster figurines one of the finest, while the organ is rightly regarded as one of the greatest in Europe, with its screen of finely fretted oak and its visible pipes made of pure tin. The care and attention given to the acoustics ensures that the quality of sound in the church is without equal, and even today the organ is in use every

Peter Macaul 73

two years in the Paisley International Organ Festival.
Nowadays the University of Paisley uses the church for its graduation
day, and it would hardly be possible to find a more imposing setting for
the ceremony than that left us by the Coats family and Hippolyte J Blanc.

Open May - Sept., Monday, Wednesday & Friday, 2 pm - 4 pm.

Q. How many gargoyles are there above the front doors?

Pedestrian route:
Exiting the church, retrace your steps along High Street, passing Paisley
Museum and Art Gallery. Turn right into New Street and turn right again
at the bottom of the hill into Shuttle Street. The next venue on the
Renfrew District Route, Sma' Shot Cottages, is on your right.

Peter Vincent 93

SMA' SHOT COTTAGES*

The expression 'Sma' Shot' probably means little to those not brought up in the fair burgh of St. Mirin, but those two little words are woven into the fabric of Paisley life in more ways than one.

The nineteenth century weavers of Paisley were considered well paid in their day, but to a man they believed they were being exploited by the manufacturers. The reason was simple. Each pass of the shuttle across the loom was termed a shot, and the weaver's wages were based on the total number of passes, but every eighth pass was of durable supporting cotton rather than the more delicate cashmere, and this was the sma' shot which the manufacturers refused to pay for. Of no help in the dispute were the 'corks' or agents, so called because they floated between the weavers and the manufacturers making a profit out of both.

So imagine the buzz of excitement that must have run through the town that day in 1856 when the employers finally relented and agreed to pay up. To the beat of the huge Charleston drum the weavers' chapels marched through the town, and in the euphoria that followed the first Saturday of July was declared an annual holiday, to be known for all time as 'Sma' Shot Day'. And so it is to this day, though there's not one weaver left in Paisley, apart of course, from the one in residence at the museum.

It was only fitting therefore when the Old Paisley Society acquired a row of 19th century mill workers' dwellings behind Shuttle Street, that they should be named Sma' Shot Cottages. Now completely renovated, they act as both the Society's headquarters and a museum of old Paisley, and with the addition of a weaver's cottage just across the back court in Shuttle Street itself, they offer a unique view of the progress in the working man's living conditions over 200 years. Dating from the 1750s, the weaver's cottage gives us a glimpse of an ascetic austere life, dominated by the ever present loom, whereas the mill foreman's flat has begun to take on a few of the luxuries that we take for granted... a front room 'kept for the best', wallpaper, carpets... it may not sound much, but it is a world away from the basic weaver's cottage.

Also in the museum you will find examples of the wonderful shawls that made Paisley justly famous, as well as pots of very reasonably priced home made marmalade. Thus does the Old Paisley Society keep the identity of their fine town alive and breathing.

Open Apr - Sept., Wed & Sat 1 - 5 pm.

Q. What number is the weaver's cottage in Shuttle Street?

Pedestrian route:
Exiting Sma' Shot Cottages, turn left into Shuttle Street, and directly opposite, across New Street, you will see the next venue on the Renfrew District Route, which is the Paisley Arts Centre.

PAISLEY ARTS CENTRE

In these highly secular times, many old churches have either fallen to the bulldozer or been consigned to some totally unsuitable fate, (furniture showrooms being one favourite) but, happily, for the good Buddies of Paisley, that is not the case with their old Laigh Kirk.

Dating from 1738, this was the first church to be built in the town since the Abbey, and its simple Gothic robustness speaks of a sterner, less uncertain age. Though now almost enveloped by the bulk of a modern shopping centre, somehow it still manages to stand apart, undwarfed by materialism, and part of this air of uncompromising integrity must come from the encircling graveyard, ignored as it is by the hurrying shoppers on the concrete ramp, oblivious to the greening stones with their stark enduring messages. Among the ministers who must have preached to the occupants of the little cemetery was a certain John Witherspoon who later became the only man of the cloth to sign the American Declaration of Independence.

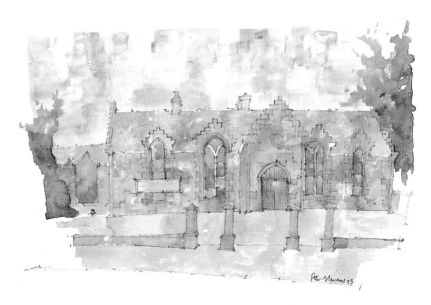

But though the souls who once trod this leafy enclave are long gone, the building they bequeathed us is very much alive, housing as it does, Paisley's Arts Centre. Opened in 1987, with its own 165 seat theatre, the centre hosts a wide selection of cultural activities ranging from straight drama and stand up comedy to avant garde dance, as well as acting as a regular venue for folk, rock, blues and jazz. With its own professional drama group aptly called PACE, who also take their productions out into the community, the Centre has become a vibrant focus for the Arts in the Paisley area. Very much in the business of encouraging indigenous talent, a large work area caters for everything from art classes and dance workshops to youth theatre, while two separate exhibition spaces provide exposure for local artists and photographers.

With its own flourishing bar and an adjacent bistro, the Centre admirably combines the roll of cultural and community centre with the commercial lightness of touch so necessary in any successful entertainment venue.

Open 7 days, 10 am till late.

Q. A round sign above the side door gives date of the church repair. When was it?

Pedestrian route:
Exiting Arts Centre, turn left into New Street then cross the main road directly into Orchard Street. At the end of Orchard Street turn left into Bridge Street crossing the White Cart Water and Abbey Close is first on the left. In Abbey Close you will find Paisley Abbey which is the last venue on the Paisley Town section of the Renfrew District Route.

PAISLEY ABBEY*

The story of Paisley Abbey is one of construction and destruction, much of it bound up with the history of the Kings of Scotland, and within the cycle can be discerned the different values which men have placed on bricks and mortar down through the centuries.

It was in 1141 that the intensely religious King David I brought Walter Fitzalan north to Scotland. A descendant of the Norman conquerors, he became the first hereditary High Steward of Scotland, receiving a castle and extensive lands in Ayrshire and Renfrewshire. He in turn set up a charter at Fotheringay, providing the lands and income for a monastery, and in 1163 brought from Shropshire an abbot and twelve monks, representing Christ and the Twelve Apostles, to found a Priory in Paisley. Fifty six years later the Priory became an Abbey, answerable only to Rome, and by the end of the 13th century it was serving the whole of South West Scotland, bringing with it increased status to the growing town of Paisley.

The years at the turn of the 14th century were turbulent ones for the Scots Crown, as first Wallace then Bruce grappled with the army of Edward I till, in 1307, the 'Hammer of the Scots' lost patience with his insubordinate neighbours and set fire to the great Abbey. All through the 1300s, while War and pestilence decimated the population, restoration continued. Six High Stewards were buried here, as was Marjory Bruce, daughter of Robert the Bruce, mother of Robert II, first of the Royal Stewarts. A memorial to her is now in the choir, and close to it on the wall is a plaque with the list of High Stewards interred here.

Then in 1570, even as the first winds of the Reformation were beginning to blow through Scotland, the cycle turned once again to destruction as the central tower collapsed, taking with it the roofs and upper walls of the North Transept, Crossing and Choir. And so the dismembered church was to stay for the next 350 years. Now with a new wall across the nave, the truncated space serves as a parish church of the Church of Scotland. It was not till the second half of the 19th century that a gradual process of repair was begun, a process which culminated in 1928 with the reopening of the Choir, now rebuilt and re-roofed. And so the Abbey survives, its rebirth continuing with the addition of a new timber roof in the nave in 1981 and repairs to the tower begun in 1993.

Open daily 10 am - 3.30 pm.

Q. Which two saints are depicted on the small wooden entrance door?

Route:
You are now directly opposite Paisley Town Hall, and have therefore completed the Paisley Town section of the Renfrew District Route. To visit the other venues on the route return to your car and proceed up Paisley High Street until it merges with Ferguslie which is the main Johnstone Road. Continue along the road into the village of Elderslie (about 2 1/4 miles in total). Just past the Gulf petrol station on your left you will find the next venue on the Renfrew District Route which is the Wallace Monument.

WALLACE MONUMENT

On a tree lined wedge of grass just off the busy Paisley to Johnstone road stands a monument to a man who had no grave, and on one of the bronze plaques round its base is the reason why.

It was Wallace's misfortune to live during the reign of England's expansionist king, Edward I, who dreamt of uniting the island under one rule, but it was due mainly to Wallace that Edward died with his ambitions thwarted. Born around 1270, little is known of his early life, but symbolically it was the slaying of an insulting Englishman which propelled him from anonymity. Outlawed and forced to go on the run, he collected round about him a band of like minded men, and began his life's work, which can be described succinctly as resisting the English. By 1284, Edward had already conquered Wales, presenting the Principality to his heir, and after sorting out some problems with his French possessions in Gascony, he was ready to turn his attention to Scotland. Meanwhile Wallace's followers had grown steadily, and despite the fickleness of the Scots nobles, who had a habit of deserting at the first sign of enemy activity, the country was in a virtual state of insurrection. When at last the showdown came, on September 11, 1297 at the Battle of Stirling Bridge, it was to prove his greatest triumph. The English army was all but destroyed, and in the aftermath Wallace devastated the northern part of England as far south as Newcastle and was elected guardian of Scotland.

But the victory was to be short-lived. In the following year Edward marched north with a much larger army and inflicted a crushing defeat on the Scots. Wallace was forced to take to the mountains, and for the next seven years he waged a guerilla campaign against the English, but finally he was captured near Glasgow and was taken in chains to London. Tried and condemned as a traitor, he was hung drawn and quartered in Smithfield on August 23, 1305 and the parts of his body were displayed in various areas of Edward's new Empire as warning to others. Hence no grave.

So this granite obelisk stands near his reputed birthplace, its central column dominated by a long sword enwrapped by a swirling wreath, a memorial to the man who inspired his countrymen to fight to the death rather than accept subjugation. Happily, just a few short years after

Wallace's barbaric execution, Robert the Bruce was to make sure that future generations of Scots would have no need to face that terrible choice.

Q. One of the bronze plaques on the base is a replica, where is the original?

Route:
Leaving the Wallace monument, continue along the A737 into Johnstone. Follow signs for the Town Centre, B879, (right fork). Pass the bandstands on Johnstone main square, straight through at traffic lights then at first roundabout take a left turn, and go down the ramp onto the A737 dual carriageway heading towards Irvine. Kilbarchan is the first exit off the A737. Exiting up ramp to a T-junction, turn right, and follow signposts for Kilbarchan, straight through two mini roundabouts. Proceed along Low Barholm, and turn right into Ewing Street as the new road begins to skirt the old village. At the top of Ewing Street you will see the next venue on the Renfrew District Route, which is Kilbarchan Hall.

KILBARCHAN HALL*

If you'd like to know what the inhabitants of Kilbarchan have in common with a stanza form used by Robert Burns read on.

There is something delightfully human about the scale of Kilbarchan's Steeple. Built in 1755 by David Kerr, a local master stonemason, it doubled as a school and market, and it has a size that relates directly to its function. The building has a solid feel, the lines of its squat stone spire clean and uncluttered, and the sum of the parts somehow resonates with its surrounding grass and trees. But what makes the building really unique is the statue of the piper in the central niche of the tripartite Palladian feature above the front door.

Habbie Simpson, the Kilbarchan piper, was born early in the 16th century, and as a young herdsman he saved four Scots pounds from his wages to buy his first 'stand' of bagpipes. In those pre-Reformation days, the piper was at the heart of a Scottish culture which still observed many rituals dating back to Celtic times. At weddings the piper would play a tune called 'Maidin-trace' as he led the bride and her maidens south-wards three times round the Church (never northwards, this being Widdershins, and associated with Sorcery) while among the many feasts that were still being celebrated in Habbie's day was Beltane, the original Celtic Mayday.

All of this would have changed with the Reformation, for Scottish Protestantism had an abhorrence of feast days and festivals which extended even to the celebration of Christmas. But there were still secular festivities, like Kilbarchan's annual horse race, and it was here on Pennel Green that there occurred the famous incident when some joker stabbed Habbie's windbag, letting out all the air, and promptly received the same treatment from the piper's dagger. Luckily for both, however, the sheath was still on, though due to a small libation Habbie failed to notice this and fearing reprisals from the man's family, had to lay low for a few days at Linwood Moss.

We know that Habbie lived to a ripe old age, for we have him 'teethless, auld and teuch', in the poem by Robert Sempill which was to help make the Kilbarchan Piper immortal. Sempill was a local landowner who lived for the first sixty years of the 17th century, and it was his 'Elegy on Habbie Simpson' which in 1822 inspired Archibald Robertson of Greenock to make the wooden statue which originally graced the Steeple Hall niche. (The present bronze copy dates from 1932).

And the riddle? Well, Sempill's distinctive stanza form in the Elegy, with its two added short lines, was to become known as Standard Habbie, later used by Burns and Ramsay, and by a similar process of osmosis, the inhabitants of this most distinctive of Renfrewshire villages have come to be known as Habbies. All of which would no doubt have delighted their famous namesake.

Q. According to the plaque on the front door when was the Kilbarchan General Society instituted?

Route:

Leaving the Steeple Hall, proceed down Steeple Street and directly ahead of you, across the main road, you will see the next venue on the Renfrew District Route which is the Kilbarchan Weaver's Cottage.

KILBARCHAN WEAVER'S COTTAGE

For a village so close to the ever expanding urban complex, Kilbarchan
has somehow managed to retain not only its unique charm, but also its
sense of identity and the credit for that must surely be due to the weavers.

The quintessential cottage industry of weaving characterised Kilbarchan
for in its heyday in the 1830s there were 800 looms in the village, every
household with its own, and every member of the family expected to do
his or her bit in the process. Amazingly, remnants of that way of life hung
on till well into the 1950s, but when that last generation of master
weavers died out the skill all but went with them, and now all that remains
of a once thriving industry is the Weaver's Cottage at the Cross, run by
the National Trust for Scotland. The cottage itself was built in 1723 by
the Bryden family, and in its original smaller version would have been
typical of the whole village. What we have now is two adjacent cottages,
united with a room upstairs in the roof space. This affords an excellent
view of the 'cruck' system of building, where the weight of the roof was
carried by a framework of curved tree trunks, in an unlikely anticipation

of the modern steel frame system of building. Other features of interest are the box beds in the room recesses, and in the kitchen a traditional black hob grate.

As basic as life would have been, working at home on a hand loom would surely have been preferable to drudgery in the factories of Paisley. And while Paisley paid the price of over-specialisation at the end of the 19th century when the shawl went out of fashion, Kilbarchan's weavers continued for another fifty years producing tartans for the army and ponchos for the Americas. Weavers like Willie Meikle, were known the world over; among his customers royalty of three generations.

Willie's presence seems to fill the little house and it is his loom you will find in the basement, with the typical depression in the floor to take the pedals. His portrait smiles wryly from the wall and among the exhibits you will find on show are some of his tools, his tartan waistcoat and trousers. Before he died Willie passed the skill on to the next generation so the loom continues to weave tartans in the museum, keeping Kilbarchan's heritage alive in more than a purely symbolic way.

Open Good Friday - Easter Monday 1.30 - 5.30 pm, 9th - 30th April and 1st - 23rd October Saturday and Sunday 1.30 - 5.30 pm. 1st May to 30th September 1.30 - 5.30 pm.

Q. According to the inscription above the door, when was the cottage 'builded'?

Route:
Exiting the cottage, turn right down Church Street till you reach the T-junction. Turn right into Burntshields Road following signpost for Lochwinnoch, and follow this delightful twisting country road for almost three miles till on the left you see the huge Clochodrick Stone. Turn left just after this and proceed to the T-junction, turn right and then left into the B786 signposted Lochwinnoch. Follow road till you enter Lochwinnoch, proceed along the narrow Main Street over the bridge across the River Calder, then turn immediately left at the T-junction into the A760. Further along this road you will see the signpost for the next venue on the Renfrew District Route, which is the Royal Society for the Protection of Bird's Lochwinnoch Nature Reserve.

ROYAL SOCIETY FOR THE PROTECTION OF BIRDS LOCHWINNOCH

With an increasing percentage of Scotland's wetlands under environmental pressure the role of sanctuaries like the one at Lochwinnoch becomes that bit more important.

Lochwinnoch reserve was established in 1974 covering an area of 580 acres comprising marshland and open water which had been the subject of a large drainage scheme in the early 1800s. When this was finally abandoned in the 1950s, the area gradually returned to marshland, providing ideal nesting conditions among the reeds and sedges along the water's edge, and to date over 170 species of birds have been recorded on the reserve, of which 66 have actually bred.

The nature centre with its observation tower was opened in 1978, and from it you can see the two trails stretching out like a horseshoe round the edge of the loch, each with its own hides. The shorter of the two is Dubbs trail, and from the hide at its end you may be lucky enough in Spring to see the great crested grebes carrying their young on their back to protect them from underwater predators like the pike. Normally the food chain moves in the opposite direction, with the loch providing plentiful food for the birds, but the waters are also home to eels, roach and three-spined sticklebacks, as well as a family of otters.

Winter sees the arrival of the Greylag geese and Whooper swans, together with large numbers of shovellers and teals, but it is in summertime that the reserve is at its splendid best, with the marsh marigolds splashing yellow through the golden reeds and damselflies and dragonflies skimming across the open waters.

Open every day, 10 am - 5 pm.

Q. What does the Dubbs Water Trail overlook?

Route:
Exiting the Nature Centre, turn right back into the A760, then 2nd right into the B786 signposted Kilmacolm. Proceed back through Lochwin-noch, staying on this road all the way till you enter Kilmacolm on the Lochwinnoch Road. When you reach a set of crossroads, go straight through into Market Place which swings to the left and becomes High Street. Continue up High Street and take third right into West Glen Road. Follow this road for 3.5 miles until you reach a T-junction. Turn left and after half a mile you will see a signpost pointing right, directing you to Formakin Estate. Turn right and a few hundred metres along on the left hand side you will find Formakin Estate, which is the last venue on the Renfrew District Route.

FORMAKIN ESTATE

Enter Formakin Estate through the two imposing gatehouses and you are in a world once exclusively reserved for the landed gentry. The grandeur of the stately Scots Baronial mansion peering out across wooded parkland speaks of generations of aristocratic breeding, centuries of continuity, as indeed does the date inscribed above the arch into the stable courtyard.. 1693.. but wait a minute! What about the letters D L just underneath? Is that the family initials? Well actually, no. They sum up what you're seeing, and they stand for 'damned lie'!! The truth is, if you'd passed this way a century ago, you'd have found nothing but an old mill and some good farmland, which is what a certain stockbroker by the name of John Augustus Holms did. Johnny was a wealthy chap who had amassed a rather large art collection and was keen to find somewhere worthy of housing it, but as those were the days when the old moneyed classes still had some and country estates were hard to come by, our Mr. Holms set out to build his own.

The land was duly bought and lovingly converted into a succession of formal gardens each with its own theme, replete with rare species of plants and flowers. Unusually for a stockbroker, nature was actually Holms' greatest passion and in the grounds of Formakin it was given full vent. Blue Himalayan poppies vied for attention with snowdrops, peonies and creamy magnolias, while the mill buildings played backdrop to a host of yellow mahonias.

Up at the big house construction was moving apace, with the architect Robert Lorimer taking the Holms dictum that money was no object to literal extremes, when the inevitable happened. Due, it would seem, to a partner's bad dealing, the money abruptly ran out. With £60,000 spent on labour and building materials, and the house all but complete, all work stopped. The dream ended... But not quite. Holms spent the rest of his life at Formakin, and though without electricity or water the mansion was never lived in, he did manage to hold the odd dinner party in a room off the great hall, candlelight picking out the detritus of the builders who had downed tools on that fateful day. He grew flowers and shrubs and sold his horticultural specimens, gaining in the meantime a reputation for eccentricity enhanced by his penchant for chasing anyone caught stealing flowers off the estate. When he died in 1938 the remnants of his collection were auctioned off to pay his debts, and the estate was bought by A.E. Pickard another famous Glasgow eccentric, who let the estate grow wild.

Now, saved from decay and lovingly restored by the Formakin trust, the estate is at last becoming what Holms dreamt it would be, and the wonderful gardens with their own magically peaceful atmosphere are surely as he would have wished them to be, serving as a lasting tribute to a most untypical stockbroker.

Open 11 am - 6 pm every day. Adults £1.50, Child £1.00, Family ticket £4.00.

Q. What stone animals inhabit Formakin's courtyard roofs?

Congratulations you have now completed the Renfrew District Route. If you wish to claim your free certificate signed by the Provost, proving that you have indeed Been & Seen Renfrew District, please cut out the coupon on page 84.

Route: (Returning to Paisley Town Hall)
Exiting Formakin turn left past Bishopton cemetery. Take a right at the T-junction into Bishopton. At next T-junction turn right onto the main A8 road, passing the Bishopton Inn on your right hand side. Go through roundabout, (2nd exit), signposted Inchinnan, and continue to a set of traffic lights just over a hump backed bridge. Take a hard right (signposted Paisley), continuing round perimeter of Glasgow Airport. At roundabout take first exit left, marked Paisley. This road becomes Love Street at the end of which you will join the one way system flowing left. Follow sign right for Town Centre into New Sneddon Street. Cross the traffic lights into Gilmour Street. Then turn left into High Street / Gauze Street and you are back at Paisley Town Hall which is just over the bridge across the river Cart.

Write your Renfrew District answers here:

Paisley Town Hall:..

Coats Observatory:..

Paisley Museum:...

Coats Memorial Church:...

Sma' Shot Cottages:..

Paisley Arts Centre:...

Paisley Abbey:..

Wallace Monument:...

Kilbarchan Hall:..

Weaver's Cottage:...

RSPB Lochwinnoch:...

Formakin Estate:...

To claim your free certificate proving that you have indeed Been and Seen the District of Renfrew, please complete the coupon below answering all the questions, cut along the dotted line and send it in an envelope to:

Tourism Executive
Renfrewshire Enterprise
27 Causeyside Street
Paisley
PA1 1UL

I have visited all twelve venues on the Renfrew District Route.

Signed...

Witnessed by..

PLEASE PRINT DETAILS BELOW CLEARLY IN BLACK INK

Name...Age......

Address...

....

....

Postcode........................ Country...................................

Which venue did you best like...

Which venue did you least like..

During your visit where did you stay overnight: (please tick)
Home ..... Friends/ Relatives ..... Bed & Breakfast ..... Camping ....
Hotel ..... Caravan ..... Youth Hostel ..... Self catering ..... Other ....

What is the main purpose of your visit to Renfrew District?
Part of a holiday, weekend or short break ..... Conference .....
On business: staying overnight ..... daytrip .....
Visiting friends / relatives ..... On a day trip or short visit from home ..... To take part in the Renfrew District Route .....

Overall how would you rate the venues? much better than you expected ..... a bit better than expected ..... much as expected ..... a bit disappointing ..... very disappointing .....

Did you feel welcome in Renfrew District? Yes ..... No .....

Would you visit Renfrew District again? Yes..... No.....

Would you recommend Renfrew District to friends? Yes ..... No .....

What in your opinion is Renfrew District's best asset?...................

....

Please describe Renfrew District in one word...........................

Thank you for taking the time to answer the questions.

Renfrew District Route Overview

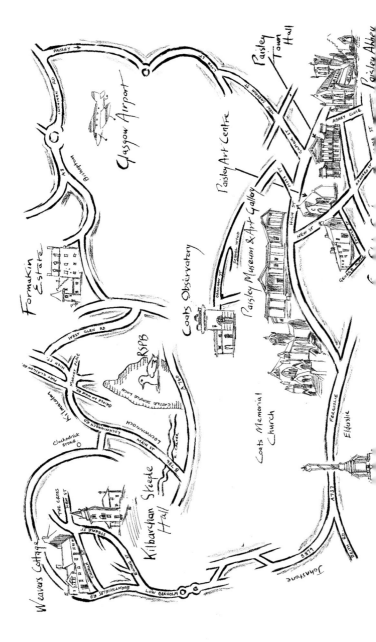

The venues marked with an * in the Renfrew District section are now available as signed, limited edition prints. If you wish to order please complete and send the coupon below to:

Been & Seen Publishing
PO Box 821 Gourock
Renfrewshire PA19 1LP
Scotland

Name..

Address..

....

....

Postcode..................Phone Number..........................

Please tick the print / s you wish to order

Please send me the following signed, limited edition print / s:

Sma' Shot Cottages   ....
Paisley Abbey   ....
Kilbarchan Hall   ....
Coats Memorial Church   ....

The size of each print is 296 x 420 mm. The cost of each print is £7.95. There is a limit of 850 signed numbered copies of each and orders will be dispatched on a strictly first come first served basis. Each print is signed and numbered by the award winning artist Peter A. Michael. Please add £0.95 for packaging and delivery per order. UK only. Please add £2.60 for packaging and delivery per order overseas. The above price of £7.95 includes VAT at 17.5%. Cheques payable to Been & Seen Publishing or alternatively please debit my credit card.

Access / Visa card number _ _ _ _ _ _ _ _ _ _ _ _ _ _ _ _

Expiry date _ _ / _ _ Signature_ _ _ _ _ _ _ _ _ _ _ _ _ _

Please allow 21 days for order processing and delivery.